MW01519790

Name	Phone	Email

MEDICATION RECORD

Date: _____   Pain Level: _____

MEDICATION / DOSE	TIME	TIME	TIME	TIME

EXERCISE CHART

Water: ☐ ☐ ☐ ☐ ☐ ☐ ☐ ☐ ☐ ☐

TIME	EXERCISE NAME (OR ICE)	REPS (or MINUTES)

MEDICATION RECORD

Date: _____   Pain Level: _____

MEDICATION / DOSE	TIME	TIME	TIME	TIME

EXERCISE CHART

Water: ☐ ☐ ☐ ☐ ☐ ☐ ☐ ☐ ☐ ☐

TIME	EXERCISE NAME (OR ICE)	REPS (or MINUTES)

MEDICATION RECORD

Date: _____   Pain Level: _____

MEDICATION / DOSE	TIME	TIME	TIME	TIME

EXERCISE CHART

Water: ☐ ☐ ☐ ☐ ☐ ☐ ☐ ☐ ☐ ☐

TIME	EXERCISE NAME (OR ICE)	REPS (or MINUTES)

MEDICATION RECORD

Date: _____   Pain Level: _____

MEDICATION / DOSE	TIME	TIME	TIME	TIME

EXERCISE CHART

Water: ☐ ☐ ☐ ☐ ☐ ☐ ☐ ☐ ☐ ☐

TIME	EXERCISE NAME (OR ICE)	REPS (or MINUTES)

MEDICATION RECORD

Date: _____   Pain Level: _____

MEDICATION / DOSE	TIME	TIME	TIME	TIME

EXERCISE CHART

Water: ☐ ☐ ☐ ☐ ☐ ☐ ☐ ☐ ☐ ☐

TIME	EXERCISE NAME (OR ICE)	REPS (or MINUTES)

MEDICATION RECORD

Date: _____   Pain Level: _____

MEDICATION / DOSE	TIME	TIME	TIME	TIME

EXERCISE CHART

Water: ☐ ☐ ☐ ☐ ☐ ☐ ☐ ☐ ☐ ☐

TIME	EXERCISE NAME (OR ICE)	REPS (or MINUTES)

MEDICATION RECORD

Date: _____   Pain Level: _____

MEDICATION / DOSE	TIME	TIME	TIME	TIME

EXERCISE CHART

Water: ☐ ☐ ☐ ☐ ☐ ☐ ☐ ☐ ☐ ☐

TIME	EXERCISE NAME (OR ICE)	REPS (or MINUTES)

MEDICATION RECORD

Date: _____   Pain Level: _____

MEDICATION / DOSE	TIME	TIME	TIME	TIME

EXERCISE CHART

Water: ☐ ☐ ☐ ☐ ☐ ☐ ☐ ☐ ☐ ☐

TIME	EXERCISE NAME (OR ICE)	REPS (or MINUTES)

MEDICATION RECORD

Date: _____   Pain Level: _____

MEDICATION / DOSE	TIME	TIME	TIME	TIME

EXERCISE CHART

Water: ☐ ☐ ☐ ☐ ☐ ☐ ☐ ☐ ☐ ☐

TIME	EXERCISE NAME (OR ICE)	REPS (or MINUTES)

MEDICATION RECORD

Date: _____   Pain Level: _____

MEDICATION / DOSE	TIME	TIME	TIME	TIME

EXERCISE CHART

Water: ☐ ☐ ☐ ☐ ☐ ☐ ☐ ☐ ☐ ☐

TIME	EXERCISE NAME (OR ICE)	REPS (or MINUTES)

MEDICATION RECORD

Date: _____   Pain Level: _____

MEDICATION / DOSE	TIME	TIME	TIME	TIME

EXERCISE CHART

Water: ☐ ☐ ☐ ☐ ☐ ☐ ☐ ☐ ☐ ☐

TIME	EXERCISE NAME (OR ICE)	REPS (or MINUTES)

MEDICATION RECORD

Date: _____   Pain Level: _____

MEDICATION / DOSE	TIME	TIME	TIME	TIME

EXERCISE CHART

Water: ☐ ☐ ☐ ☐ ☐ ☐ ☐ ☐ ☐ ☐

TIME	EXERCISE NAME (OR ICE)	REPS (or MINUTES)

MEDICATION RECORD

Date: _____   Pain Level: _____

MEDICATION / DOSE	TIME	TIME	TIME	TIME

EXERCISE CHART

Water: ☐ ☐ ☐ ☐ ☐ ☐ ☐ ☐ ☐ ☐

TIME	EXERCISE NAME (OR ICE)	REPS (or MINUTES)

MEDICATION RECORD

Date: _____   Pain Level: _____

MEDICATION / DOSE	TIME	TIME	TIME	TIME

EXERCISE CHART

Water: ☐ ☐ ☐ ☐ ☐ ☐ ☐ ☐ ☐ ☐

TIME	EXERCISE NAME (OR ICE)	REPS (or MINUTES)

MEDICATION RECORD

Date: _____   Pain Level: _____

MEDICATION / DOSE	TIME	TIME	TIME	TIME

EXERCISE CHART

Water: ☐ ☐ ☐ ☐ ☐ ☐ ☐ ☐ ☐ ☐

TIME	EXERCISE NAME (OR ICE)	REPS (or MINUTES)

MEDICATION RECORD

Date: _____   Pain Level: _____

MEDICATION / DOSE	TIME	TIME	TIME	TIME

EXERCISE CHART

Water: ☐ ☐ ☐ ☐ ☐ ☐ ☐ ☐ ☐ ☐

TIME	EXERCISE NAME (OR ICE)	REPS (or MINUTES)

MEDICATION RECORD

Date: _____   Pain Level: _____

MEDICATION / DOSE	TIME	TIME	TIME	TIME

EXERCISE CHART

Water: ☐ ☐ ☐ ☐ ☐ ☐ ☐ ☐ ☐ ☐

TIME	EXERCISE NAME (OR ICE)	REPS (or MINUTES)

MEDICATION RECORD

Date: _____   Pain Level: _____

MEDICATION / DOSE	TIME	TIME	TIME	TIME

EXERCISE CHART

Water: ☐ ☐ ☐ ☐ ☐ ☐ ☐ ☐ ☐ ☐

TIME	EXERCISE NAME (OR ICE)	REPS (or MINUTES)

MEDICATION RECORD

Date: _____   Pain Level: _____

MEDICATION / DOSE	TIME	TIME	TIME	TIME

EXERCISE CHART

Water: ☐ ☐ ☐ ☐ ☐ ☐ ☐ ☐ ☐ ☐

TIME	EXERCISE NAME (OR ICE)	REPS (or MINUTES)

MEDICATION RECORD

Date: _____   Pain Level: _____

MEDICATION / DOSE	TIME	TIME	TIME	TIME

EXERCISE CHART

Water: ☐ ☐ ☐ ☐ ☐ ☐ ☐ ☐ ☐ ☐

TIME	EXERCISE NAME (OR ICE)	REPS (or MINUTES)

MEDICATION RECORD

Date: _____   Pain Level: _____

MEDICATION / DOSE	TIME	TIME	TIME	TIME

EXERCISE CHART

Water: ☐ ☐ ☐ ☐ ☐ ☐ ☐ ☐ ☐ ☐

TIME	EXERCISE NAME (OR ICE)	REPS (or MINUTES)

MEDICATION RECORD

Date: _____   Pain Level: _____

MEDICATION / DOSE	TIME	TIME	TIME	TIME

EXERCISE CHART

Water: ☐ ☐ ☐ ☐ ☐ ☐ ☐ ☐ ☐ ☐

TIME	EXERCISE NAME (OR ICE)	REPS (or MINUTES)

MEDICATION RECORD

Date: _____   Pain Level: _____

MEDICATION / DOSE	TIME	TIME	TIME	TIME

EXERCISE CHART

Water: ☐ ☐ ☐ ☐ ☐ ☐ ☐ ☐ ☐ ☐

TIME	EXERCISE NAME (OR ICE)	REPS (or MINUTES)

MEDICATION RECORD

Date: _____   Pain Level: _____

MEDICATION / DOSE	TIME	TIME	TIME	TIME

EXERCISE CHART

Water: ☐ ☐ ☐ ☐ ☐ ☐ ☐ ☐ ☐ ☐

TIME	EXERCISE NAME (OR ICE)	REPS (or MINUTES)

MEDICATION RECORD

Date: _____   Pain Level: _____

MEDICATION / DOSE	TIME	TIME	TIME	TIME

EXERCISE CHART

Water: ☐ ☐ ☐ ☐ ☐ ☐ ☐ ☐ ☐ ☐

TIME	EXERCISE NAME (OR ICE)	REPS (or MINUTES)

MEDICATION RECORD

Date: _____   Pain Level: _____

MEDICATION / DOSE	TIME	TIME	TIME	TIME

EXERCISE CHART

Water: ☐ ☐ ☐ ☐ ☐ ☐ ☐ ☐ ☐ ☐

TIME	EXERCISE NAME (OR ICE)	REPS (or MINUTES)

MEDICATION RECORD

Date: _____   Pain Level: _____

MEDICATION / DOSE	TIME	TIME	TIME	TIME

EXERCISE CHART

Water: ☐ ☐ ☐ ☐ ☐ ☐ ☐ ☐ ☐ ☐

TIME	EXERCISE NAME (OR ICE)	REPS (or MINUTES)

MEDICATION RECORD

Date: _____   Pain Level: _____

MEDICATION / DOSE	TIME	TIME	TIME	TIME

EXERCISE CHART

Water: ☐ ☐ ☐ ☐ ☐ ☐ ☐ ☐ ☐ ☐

TIME	EXERCISE NAME (OR ICE)	REPS (or MINUTES)

MEDICATION RECORD

Date: _____   Pain Level: _____

MEDICATION / DOSE	TIME	TIME	TIME	TIME

EXERCISE CHART

Water: ☐ ☐ ☐ ☐ ☐ ☐ ☐ ☐ ☐ ☐

TIME	EXERCISE NAME (OR ICE)	REPS (or MINUTES)

MEDICATION RECORD

Date: _____   Pain Level: _____

MEDICATION / DOSE	TIME	TIME	TIME	TIME

EXERCISE CHART

Water: ☐ ☐ ☐ ☐ ☐ ☐ ☐ ☐ ☐ ☐

TIME	EXERCISE NAME (OR ICE)	REPS (or MINUTES)

MEDICATION RECORD

Date: _____   Pain Level: _____

MEDICATION / DOSE	TIME	TIME	TIME	TIME

EXERCISE CHART

Water: ☐ ☐ ☐ ☐ ☐ ☐ ☐ ☐ ☐ ☐

TIME	EXERCISE NAME (OR ICE)	REPS (or MINUTES)

MEDICATION RECORD

Date: _____   Pain Level: _____

MEDICATION / DOSE	TIME	TIME	TIME	TIME

EXERCISE CHART

Water: ☐ ☐ ☐ ☐ ☐ ☐ ☐ ☐ ☐ ☐

TIME	EXERCISE NAME (OR ICE)	REPS (or MINUTES)

MEDICATION RECORD

Date: _____   Pain Level: _____

MEDICATION / DOSE	TIME	TIME	TIME	TIME

EXERCISE CHART

Water: ☐ ☐ ☐ ☐ ☐ ☐ ☐ ☐ ☐ ☐

TIME	EXERCISE NAME (OR ICE)	REPS (or MINUTES)

MEDICATION RECORD

Date: _____   Pain Level: _____

MEDICATION / DOSE	TIME	TIME	TIME	TIME

EXERCISE CHART

Water: ☐ ☐ ☐ ☐ ☐ ☐ ☐ ☐ ☐ ☐

TIME	EXERCISE NAME (OR ICE)	REPS (or MINUTES)

MEDICATION RECORD

Date: _____   Pain Level: _____

MEDICATION / DOSE	TIME	TIME	TIME	TIME

EXERCISE CHART

Water: ☐ ☐ ☐ ☐ ☐ ☐ ☐ ☐ ☐ ☐

TIME	EXERCISE NAME (OR ICE)	REPS (or MINUTES)

MEDICATION RECORD

Date: _____ Pain Level: _____

MEDICATION / DOSE	TIME	TIME	TIME	TIME

EXERCISE CHART

Water: ☐ ☐ ☐ ☐ ☐ ☐ ☐ ☐ ☐ ☐

TIME	EXERCISE NAME (OR ICE)	REPS (or MINUTES)

MEDICATION RECORD

Date: _____   Pain Level: _____

MEDICATION / DOSE	TIME	TIME	TIME	TIME

EXERCISE CHART

Water: ☐ ☐ ☐ ☐ ☐ ☐ ☐ ☐ ☐ ☐

TIME	EXERCISE NAME (OR ICE)	REPS (or MINUTES)

MEDICATION RECORD

Date: _____   Pain Level: _____

MEDICATION / DOSE	TIME	TIME	TIME	TIME

EXERCISE CHART

Water: ☐ ☐ ☐ ☐ ☐ ☐ ☐ ☐ ☐ ☐

TIME	EXERCISE NAME (OR ICE)	REPS (or MINUTES)

MEDICATION RECORD

Date: _____   Pain Level: _____

MEDICATION / DOSE	TIME	TIME	TIME	TIME

EXERCISE CHART

Water: ☐ ☐ ☐ ☐ ☐ ☐ ☐ ☐ ☐ ☐

TIME	EXERCISE NAME (OR ICE)	REPS (or MINUTES)

MEDICATION RECORD

Date: _____   Pain Level: _____

MEDICATION / DOSE	TIME	TIME	TIME	TIME

EXERCISE CHART

Water: ☐ ☐ ☐ ☐ ☐ ☐ ☐ ☐ ☐ ☐

TIME	EXERCISE NAME (OR ICE)	REPS (or MINUTES)

MEDICATION RECORD

Date: _____   Pain Level: _____

MEDICATION / DOSE	TIME	TIME	TIME	TIME

EXERCISE CHART

Water: ☐ ☐ ☐ ☐ ☐ ☐ ☐ ☐ ☐ ☐

TIME	EXERCISE NAME (OR ICE)	REPS (or MINUTES)

MEDICATION RECORD

Date: _____   Pain Level: _____

MEDICATION / DOSE	TIME	TIME	TIME	TIME

EXERCISE CHART

Water: ☐ ☐ ☐ ☐ ☐ ☐ ☐ ☐ ☐ ☐

TIME	EXERCISE NAME (OR ICE)	REPS (or MINUTES)

MEDICATION RECORD

Date: _____   Pain Level: _____

MEDICATION / DOSE	TIME	TIME	TIME	TIME

EXERCISE CHART

Water: ☐ ☐ ☐ ☐ ☐ ☐ ☐ ☐ ☐ ☐

TIME	EXERCISE NAME (OR ICE)	REPS (or MINUTES)

MEDICATION RECORD

Date: _____   Pain Level: _____

MEDICATION / DOSE	TIME	TIME	TIME	TIME

EXERCISE CHART

Water: ☐ ☐ ☐ ☐ ☐ ☐ ☐ ☐ ☐ ☐

TIME	EXERCISE NAME (OR ICE)	REPS (or MINUTES)

MEDICATION RECORD

Date: _____   Pain Level: _____

MEDICATION / DOSE	TIME	TIME	TIME	TIME

EXERCISE CHART

Water: ☐ ☐ ☐ ☐ ☐ ☐ ☐ ☐ ☐ ☐

TIME	EXERCISE NAME (OR ICE)	REPS (or MINUTES)

MEDICATION RECORD

Date: _____   Pain Level: _____

MEDICATION / DOSE	TIME	TIME	TIME	TIME

EXERCISE CHART

Water: ☐ ☐ ☐ ☐ ☐ ☐ ☐ ☐ ☐ ☐

TIME	EXERCISE NAME (OR ICE)	REPS (or MINUTES)

MEDICATION RECORD

Date: _____   Pain Level: _____

MEDICATION / DOSE	TIME	TIME	TIME	TIME

EXERCISE CHART

Water: ☐ ☐ ☐ ☐ ☐ ☐ ☐ ☐ ☐ ☐

TIME	EXERCISE NAME (OR ICE)	REPS (or MINUTES)

MEDICATION RECORD

Date: _____   Pain Level: _____

MEDICATION / DOSE	TIME	TIME	TIME	TIME

EXERCISE CHART

Water: ☐ ☐ ☐ ☐ ☐ ☐ ☐ ☐ ☐ ☐

TIME	EXERCISE NAME (OR ICE)	REPS (or MINUTES)

MEDICATION RECORD

Date: _____   Pain Level: _____

MEDICATION / DOSE	TIME	TIME	TIME	TIME

EXERCISE CHART

Water: ☐ ☐ ☐ ☐ ☐ ☐ ☐ ☐ ☐ ☐

TIME	EXERCISE NAME (OR ICE)	REPS (or MINUTES)

MEDICATION RECORD

Date: _____   Pain Level: _____

MEDICATION / DOSE	TIME	TIME	TIME	TIME

EXERCISE CHART

Water: ☐ ☐ ☐ ☐ ☐ ☐ ☐ ☐ ☐

TIME	EXERCISE NAME (OR ICE)	REPS (or MINUTES)

MEDICATION RECORD

Date: _____   Pain Level: _____

MEDICATION / DOSE	TIME	TIME	TIME	TIME

EXERCISE CHART

Water: ☐ ☐ ☐ ☐ ☐ ☐ ☐ ☐ ☐ ☐

TIME	EXERCISE NAME (OR ICE)	REPS (or MINUTES)

MEDICATION RECORD

Date: _____   Pain Level: _____

MEDICATION / DOSE	TIME	TIME	TIME	TIME

EXERCISE CHART

Water: ☐ ☐ ☐ ☐ ☐ ☐ ☐ ☐ ☐ ☐

TIME	EXERCISE NAME (OR ICE)	REPS (or MINUTES)

MEDICATION RECORD

Date: _____   Pain Level: _____

MEDICATION / DOSE	TIME	TIME	TIME	TIME

EXERCISE CHART

Water: ☐ ☐ ☐ ☐ ☐ ☐ ☐ ☐ ☐ ☐

TIME	EXERCISE NAME (OR ICE)	REPS (or MINUTES)

MEDICATION RECORD

Date: _____   Pain Level: _____

MEDICATION / DOSE	TIME	TIME	TIME	TIME

EXERCISE CHART

Water: ☐ ☐ ☐ ☐ ☐ ☐ ☐ ☐ ☐ ☐

TIME	EXERCISE NAME (OR ICE)	REPS (or MINUTES)

Manufactured by Amazon.ca
Bolton, ON